To

all best

wishes.

Paul

2

March

1997

A unique, illustrated book*
of humor and
insightful commentary.

*This book loves coffee tables.

TOADS

Paul B. Lowney

Drawings by Frank Renlie

CROWNE AND LURIE PUBLISHERS

Copyright 1996 Paul B. Lowney, Seattle, Washington
All rights reserved
ISBN 0-9609946-3-7
Library of Congress Catalog Card Number: 96-85739
Printed in the United States of America

*Dedicated to Laura, who is old enough
to understand most of
this book, but not old enough to
understand all of it.*

Foreword

*A*fter my hard-cover, *The Best in Offbeat Humor II*, came off the press early this year, I said to the book's illustrator, Frank Renlie: "This is my last book. I have nothing more to offer." Frank, a longtime associate who illustrated five of my *Gleeb* books, replied: "I've heard this song before. You'll do another one."

Frank was right. Two weeks later I phoned and said: "I have a great idea for another book. I'll use condensed versions of pieces from *Gleeb*, and I'll add bits I wrote for *Reader's Digest*, plus a lot of new material. We'll load the book with your drawings – probably humanoid animal characters – and we'll call the book either *Toads* or *Stikles*."

Without a second of hesitation, Frank said: "I like *Toads*."

Much of the writing in this book is characterized by the words of a *Saturday Review* columnist who commented on one of my early books, *No Charge for Dreaming*: "...Lowney makes you think and then laugh and sometimes makes you laugh and then think." I like that observation.

Some of the following pieces are humorous and some are serious and some are both humorous and serious. Readers who look for a humorous point in every offering will end up with: "I don't get it."

I would not have attempted this book without the talent of Frank Renlie to give visual life to my words with his imaginative and stylized graphics. The reader can think of this volume as a book of writing supported by drawings or a book of drawings supported by writing.

Invariably the question arises as it does with all writers: "Where do you get your ideas?" My answer is always the same: "I get my ideas while shaving. This trait must run in the family. My daughter gets her ideas while putting on her makeup."

Enjoy the following pages. If there are pieces in here you like, please let me know. If there are pieces in here you don't like, please don't bother.

PAUL B. LOWNEY
1996

Make a mental note of that, and if the note doesn't suit you, tear it up.

Is this the real you or is it Prozac, Paxil, or Zoloft?

Before I go into this party, I want to check the mirror first so I'll know how much confidence to have.

I was just rejected by someone I don't want.

Please answer three questions: 1. How small does something have to be before it doesn't exist? 2. What sort of time went on before time began? 3. If our perception of everything relies totally on our senses, and if our senses aren't reliable, then isn't it possible that the universe is only an illusion?

Laughter has no foreign accent.

Can we keep this strictly on a physical basis
until we get to know each other a little better?

I know that the four forces of nature are electromagnetism, gravity, the strong force, and the weak force; and I know that the six quarks are top, bottom, up, down, charm and strange – but I don't know what to do with this information.

You look more attractive to me now, but I'm not sure if the change is in you physically, or if it's just my perception of you, because as I grow older, it's possible I'm lowering my standards.

Many foods are both good and bad for you, so be warned: Eating can be dangerous to your health. (Not eating also can be dangerous to your health.)

The main reason for unhappiness is loneliness, and this is caused by indifference people have toward those who are socially isolated. I'd do something about this, but it's none of my business.

Why don't you have the courage of my convictions?

My friend is driving a blue car, and I know she'll be here any minute now because lately a lot of blue cars have been coming by.

In olden times, slaves made life easier for their masters. In modern times, slaves do the same, and they don't need housing or sleep, and all they eat is a little bit of electricity. They are called computers.

A visitor from another planet is easy to spot. There is no possible way to disguise an outer-space accent.

Important elements of life are health, love, status, and security, but not necessarily in that order. The order changes, depending on which elements at the moment are bringing pleasure or pain.

If life isn't giving you what you want, you have
two choices: 1. Go out in life and get what you
want. 2. Adjust your perception of life so you
believe that what you get is what you want.

Someone said to me, "Get a life!" and I said, "Where?" And that someone said, "Try the yellow pages." And I said, "What if I don't find anything?" Then the someone said, "In that case, turn yourself in; go back to the very beginning and start over – and get it right this time." At this point, there was nothing left for me to say except, "Goodbye."

21

If rabbit tastes like chicken, and if pheasant tastes like chicken, and if turtle tastes like chicken, then eat chicken.

Being in the minority is so popular nowadays, there are very few left in the majority.

There's an easy way to avoid the disastrous effects of global warming. One day a week, people on Earth could leave open their refrigerator doors.

When something annoys me, I say that something doesn't exist, and if it doesn't exist, it can't annoy me, but then something else annoys me – my self-deception.

You don't have to worry about getting involved with me. All I'm looking for is a short-term, meaningless relationship.

Space extends all the way to the end of time. I'd explain that more fully, but I don't have time.

To use the dictionary for some words, you need two dictionaries. One dictionary is for defining the word. The other is for spelling the word so you can find it in the dictionary.

From a scientific viewpoint, I can tell what it's like after we expire. It's the same as before conception – absolutely nothing. But please don't ask me to prove this by personal experience.

I forgot what I was going to say because I was listening to what you were saying instead of concentrating on what I was going to say next.

If you can't think of anything to do, you can always eat.

Occasionally, I go to socials where the people are dull and unattractive, because sometimes it's good for my ego just to stand around feeling superior.

The doctor gave me a placebo and it cured my
headache, even though I forgot to take it – but
I thought I did.

The same people who can make you happy can make you unhappy.

In life, you're more likely to get what you expect rather than what you want.

Our attitude toward life attracts the realities of life to match that attitude.

A person who keeps his word is like a rock; a person who doesn't keep his word is like a shadow.

Drinking takes the edge off of his worries, and now he's worried about his drinking.

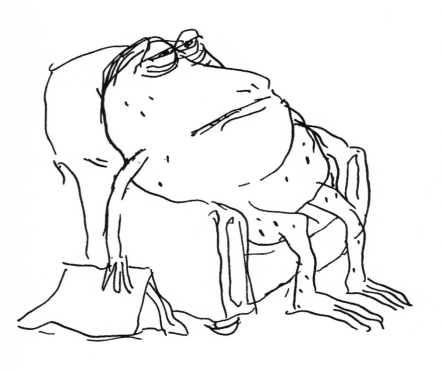

I'm sick of all the pain on this planet. I'd leave right now for another planet, but I can't – I have to work tomorrow.

He had a horn growing from his head, and he painted it pink and purple because he wanted to attract attention.

It's depressing the way she's happy all the time.

If you are overly intent on wanting something to happen, there is a good chance it won't – and if you are overly fearful something will happen, there is a good chance it will.

No one completely owns his own life. Everyone –
no matter how insignifigant – has an effect on
someone else, just as a stone sends out ripples
when thrown into still water. A person whose life
doesn't touch another's is a person without a
shadow.

When I lie to you, it hurts me, but when I tell
the truth, it's worse – it hurts you.

Don't tell me to have a nice day unless you're prepared to do something about it.

You can't always trust first impressions. Sometimes they're wrong. For instance, a woman I met irritated me a little. Later I found out differently. She irritated me a lot.

Knowing how to receive graciously is a form of giving. That's an ancient Tibetan proverb I made up this morning.

Scientific truths can be verified by precise investigation, but sociological truths are non-material and relative and hard to prove. For these truths, it takes an intelligent, logical, and objective mind such as I have – and then truth is what I say it is.

The oldest form of life are ancient bacteria about a million years old, found living, frozen in Antarctic rocks. (These bacteria will have a hard time adjusting to modern-day bacteria.) Three questions: 1. How can something be alive if it's doing absolutely nothing? 2. What exactly is it that is life? 3. Something as puny as a bacterium – why can't scientists make one?

Meditation will help you relieve stress. It works best if you're not stressed.

The science of psychoneuroimmunology tells us that affectionate touching stimulates release of endorphins and neuropetides, and this can strengthen our immune system and help protect us from illness and disease – and if you believe I'm telling you all this to take advantage of you, just think of the whole process as a kind of symbiosis.

A love relationship not capable of pain is not capable of happiness.

The only thing that can kill the mad love I have for you is your starting a mad love for me.

Let's run away together and live happily ever after – possibly longer.

In this relationship, all I ask is that you go along with one simple point: Let me make your whole life over for you.

If I knew exactly where I was going to die, I'd never go there.

The familiar saying, "You're only as old as you feel," is only half true. The other half is, "You're only as old as people around you make you feel."

A harmless lie is harmful when you're caught at it.

Fifty-two percent of the people interviewed said they believed in angels; therefore, angels exist.

You should always be kind and compassionate to animals because animals have feelings – physically and mentally – and animals are like people, except they lack higher brain function – and besides, it's possible that whatever it is that is "you" could come back in another life-time as a horse.

How was I to know that there are some truths
you don't want to hear, even when you beg to
hear them?

Dr. Bernie Siegel says, "If you don't hurt, you don't change. Pain is God's reset button."

I won't give up coffee. Why should I face life all
by myself?

Why do many people say they don't dream? What they really mean is they don't remember their dreams. It's simple to dream. I can do it in my sleep. The deeper you sleep the less you'll remember dreams, so to make certain you remember your dreams, avoid sleep.

He lived alone in the wilderness and ate animals for food, but he didn't believe in killing animals, so he taught them to commit suicide.

After I reach the top of a mountain, I feel I have conquered the mountain and that I own it, and that's probably why I try to bring it home with me.

I do not believe that life is a waste of time.

If you try and try and try and the relationship
doesn't work out, solve the problem with your
coat – put it on and clear out.

If you used any logic, you'd never marry him,
and if you are so madly in love that your logic
doesn't work, you can always use mine.

He's more cheerful now. He didn't like this world, so he made up his own.

I gave up people-watching because all the people I watched were watching me.

If you do not accept the imperfections of your loved one, you do not love at all. An old Spanish proverb.

He couldn't stand living with himself. He got
on his nerves. Several times he threatened to
move out.

Friendship growing into love can make you
happy, but love growing into friendship can
make you sad.

Let me get this straight. You're telling me that
if I lose weight, you'll take me out. Well, I have
something to tell you: If I lose weight, I can do
better than you.

There is no difference between being in love
and thinking you're in love – the joy and the
pain are the same.

The situation between Mr. Wonderful and me is this: We're just friends. And if you ask me what "friends" means, I'll tell you – it means I was dumped.

I limit my non-touch dating to Monday, Tuesday, Wednesday, Thursday, and daylight hours on Sunday.

Pursuing a losing love affair is like tightening your hand into a fist until your knuckles turn white. Letting go is like opening your hand. It feels better, but it's empty.

She's depressed because she's unhappily in love, but her friends tell her she only thinks she's in love; so, someone should give her the good news – she only thinks she's depressed.

Look for a good love, and if you can't find one, look for a good substitute.

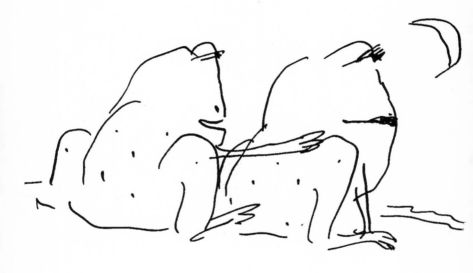

Love someone, but more important, love yourself.

You can never be on time consistently unless you risk being early.

I've decided to become happy, rich and famous, because, after all, I have to do something with my life.

The entire universe began in a vacuum with the explosion of a tiny speck of infinitely hot and dense matter, so the question is: Where did the speck come from? Since this knowledge is beyond human comprehension, the answer is: Who cares?

In my new book, I smash planet Earth into subatomic particles, but it's not that horrendous. I do it in a nice way.

For those of you who keep saying, "I need to find myself," here's a suggestion: Address a letter to yourself and then follow the postman.

On the first day of school, a teacher said to his class: "I'm Mr. Strait, your new, no-nonsense teacher. Make a note of this: Regardless of sex, race, color, creed, nationality, handicap, ethnic background, everyone in this classroom is entitled to equal punishment."

He was a disciple of the three C's – Cool Cult Conformity – and he did everything the cool and hip people did. If they wore an earring, he wore an earring; if they had a ponytail, he had a ponytail; if they wore a ballcap backwards, so did he; if they cut holes in the knees of their jeans, ditto. Someone asked him why he copied the hip and the cool people, and he answered: "Why ask me? I'm just a player on the stage of life, not the director."

Grungies who go around looking like animated litter do so for a reason – but they can't tell you what that reason is.

I'll tell you why I'm not overly impressed with the opinions of youths: I've never met an older person who ever said he knew more when he was a kid.

That kid isn't talking very much lately because he's trying to win a bet that he can go a whole month without saying "man" or "cool" or "ya know."

A student asked a wise one, "What's the meaning of life?" The wise one said, "To find out, go into the wilderness for three days – take nothing with you – and you will learn the meaning of life." The student asked, "What will I learn?" The wise one answered, "Survival."

Honesty with those you care about should not be used as a dagger to draw blood, but as a lantern to give light when darkness serves no purpose.

Some people try too hard to be themselves.

Whenever you irritate me, I eat a sandwich. Today you've irritated me a lot, so I'm going to eat four sandwiches.

The reason I paid cash for my dinner last night instead of using my credit card was that I had a miserable time with my blind date, and I didn't want to relive the whole thing in 30 days.

We should carry our friendship far enough to become a relationship, and we should carry the relationship far enough to cause pain for one of us if it ever ends.

If it's reasonable people of goodwill who decide what is "right" and what is "wrong," then the question is: Who decides what is "reasonable" and what is "goodwill"? The answer is: Reasonable people of goodwill.

Both sides demand their rights, but if granting either side its rights takes rights away from the other side, then the question is: Which side eventually gets the rights? The answer is: The side with the most power.

I no longer need treatment because I am now completely normal and well-adjusted, and if my shrink doesn't believe me, I'll punch his nose and break his glasses.

I have the talent to be a big success, but my brain locks me into a lifetime of stored data on my limitations and failures, and unless I can find a way to reprogram the stored data, you might say I'm a prisoner of my own head.

I'll go camping and rough it with you on one
condition – at night we sleep in a motel.

Suffering can teach wisdom if one has insight and understanding, but if one does not, suffering can teach something else – bitterness.

He lived a comfortable, ordinary life, not exciting and not unexciting, but he complained he was in a rut; and suddenly his whole existence was thrown into turmoil by an unexpected misfortune; and then he looked back at his life and said to himself: "It's wasn't a rut I was in – it was a groove."

Safeguard your credibility as you would precious jewels, for if you lose it, who will believe you even when you are truthful?

I've decided to become happy and well-adjusted so people won't notice how confused I am.

I'm not boastful; it's just that I have a strict rule:
I never let modesty stand in the way of the facts.

Certainly you have a right to your own opinion, but the right to an opinion doesn't ensure merit for an opinion. That's because some opinions just aren't worth a damn.

An extensive study of current studies found that many studies are flawed because of errors in compiling statistical data and because of unscientific application of controls – but a later study claimed that this particular study drew false conclusions.

I'm sorry, sir, but we have five what's-his-names
in this office.

Someone said, "Clothes make the man," but if you're familiar with the garment industry, you should know that man makes the clothes.

Of all the people who go window shopping, very few ever buy windows.

If you don't like life, search for a reasonable alternative.

If you do not spend some of your time and energy for the betterment of others, your life is not complete.

This pigeon won't fly because he thinks flying is too dangerous. Fortunately, this pigeon is an excellent walker.

What's my intention in life? In the long term – be happy and do good things. In the short term – lunch.

It's odd that people say, "It's all in your head." Certainly it's in your head. Everything you perceive in life is in your head. It's not in your big toe. If you stick a pin in your big toe, the pain is registered in you head. The next time someone says to you, "It's all in your head," you respond, "Where else do you think it is – in my big toe?"

Everyone can own a star. There are billions of
them. More than enough to go around. A star
is bright, reliable and good company – and just
pointing to it won't wear it out.

He wanted to save his terminally-ill tree by giving it a transfusion, but he couldn't find a donor with the right sap type.

I'm not fond of introductions. I'm always meeting people I don't know.

I don't believe in astrology. We Virgos are born skeptics.

He has an outstanding characteristic – he goes
unnoticed.

In the face of our distant future, we at present are ancients, and all our works are antiquities. And in the face of the distant future beyond the distant future, the same progression occurs, and so on ad infinitum. The human experience, guided by intelligence, repeated and repeated throughout thousands upon thousands of passing years, will, by its own momentum – and despite setbacks – move closer and closer to perfection until at some point in time it becomes one and intuitive with the ultimate. This could be the grand design of life.

I didn't criticize her before because before, I was in love.

A little girl fell in love with a leaf. She didn't want anyone to find her leaf, so she hid it in a tree.

When you constantly use "I'm busy" as an excuse for not doing something, what you are really saying is that the "something" is not important enough to you to make your priority list of things to get done.

A zoo is a penitentiary for animals. Their sentence: Life without parole. Their crime: Being weaker than their captors.

He isn't handsome, rich, intellectual or charis-
matic, but he has a special quality – he loves me.

I was going out to count clouds today, but I canceled because of the weather. Too cloudy.

If you're ever sucked into a black hole, you'll travel through it at the speed of light, and you won't age, but on the other hand, you won't have any fun.

In our society, a misanthrope is more socially acceptable than a bigot.

If America had lost the Revolutionary War, we'd all be speaking English today.

If you want proof that your view of life is merely a matter of perspective, consider bicycling. When you're riding a bicycle, you say to yourself, "Move your stupid cars out of my way," and when you're driving a car, you say to yourself, "Can't you find some other place to ride your dumb bicycle?"

He canceled his appointment with his psychotherapist
because he was too depressed.

If you are hesitant about going out with me because you have old problems from a broken love affair, think about it this way: I can replace your old problems with new ones.

He has a friend, but I'm sorry to say, his friend hasn't.

He didn't know if he liked the play because he hadn't read the reviews.

The antonym of synonym is antonym.

I don't respect icebergs. They have no goals. They just drift.

There are more questions about the mysteries of human life than there are answers. Consider one of the mysteries: In three billion years, how did a primitive microorganism eventually lead to a miraculous electrochemical system – the human being with the most advanced and complex organ of any life-form – the functioning human brain?

What sort of intelligence guided this long transformation from a cell to a human? We think of high intelligence emitting only from the human brain. But human intelligence didn't build the brain. Something outside of the brain did, so questions arise: Does high intelligence exist "out there" apart from the brain? Throughout the millenniums, what element, without use of a brain, constructed Earth's life systems with such intricacy that human brains cannot duplicate them or even understand why they function or what controls them?

Scientists say that humans came about through billions of years of natural selection, adaptations, and genetic mutations, but what intelligence directed these processes and provided a master blueprint?

Think about other mysteries: What super-genius source controls the functions of billions of brain cells in storing, processing, and transmitting the vital data to operate a human? Will scientists ever decipher the puzzle of how 46 microscopic chromosomes can use their chemical blueprints to activate and control the work assignments of trillions of cells for the construction of a person? And how is it possible for trillions of our body cells to hold within their minuscule nuclei the lengthy, complicated genetic code of who we are?

It took three billion years to reach all this, so we ask:

Can time do it all? Given infinite time, can time arrive at wonderous and momentous realities? Is it possible that secreted in the composition of vast stretches of time is a type of intelligence beyond the observation and understanding of the puny, finite human existence?

Perhaps infinite time has a qualitative nature as well as quantitative. For example: Explosives and machinery could remove a mountain peak in ten years, but in ten million years the element of time could remove that peak imperceptibly, grain by grain. Same results – different modes – but in a universe of infinite time, time may have the quality of spending its endless resources for reaching its own destinations and rendering only the results as ultimate realities.

In a search for answers to the mysteries, some say God did it all, and this could be so, but this raises questions for the inquiring mind: 1. Is God inexorably involved in time? 2. Three billion years to build a human? What took God so long? 3. Is there an unknowable timepiece "out there" completely out of sync with human time?

Baffled by the mysteries of life, a sage, with a tinge of humor, offered this solution: The next time someone is kidnapped by outer space aliens, have that person ask the aliens for answers to the mysteries.

A dandelion farmer found camellias growing in his field. He ripped them out and complained: "Weeds are such a nuisance."

Do not confuse being truthful with being honest. Truth is the purest form of reality. Honesty strives for truth but too often is crippled with bias.

She lies only if the truth is too painful to someone or to herself. All things considered, you can make a good case for this type of lying.

To have a good lifetime, select happy, well-adjusted, normal parents, and if that's not possible, select happy, well-adjusted, normal babysitters.

In five billion years the sun will begin running out of fuel. This thermonuclear burn-out will expand the sun 100 times its original size and will turn Earth into a scorched planetary corpse. You can make plans for this disaster right now or you can be the type who waits until the last minute.

He claimed he was the wisest one in the world. Someone asked him if God existed and he answered: "It is not important whether or not God exists. Let me explain. After humans evolved an intelligent, questioning brain, they began searching for answers to the mysteries of life surrounding them, and because this searching needed satisfaction, humans created God as a source of answers, so it mattered not whether God existed. It mattered only that the inquiring human brain found resolution in the exercise of searching and finding." And then someone asked the wise one: "Will God ever reveal himself to humans to prove He exists?" The wise one answered: "God only knows."